INSPI]

NUGGETS FOR THE

SOUL

By Karen McCann Hucks

ROYSTON
Publishing

BK Royston Publishing
P. O. Box 4321
Jeffersonville, IN 47131
502-802-5385
http://www.bkroystonpublishing.com
bkroystonpublishing@gmail.com

Cover Images: Karen Hucks
Cover Design: BK Royston Publishing LLC

ISBN: 9781729402870

Printed in the United States of America

ACKNOWLEDGMENTS

First, I must give thanks to Jesus Christ who allow me to share this special gift he has blessed me with.

This book is written to Educate, Uplift and Encourage all who read it,

This book is dedicated to my sister, Estella Marie Neal who passed away December 17, 1979, that is When I wrote my first poem because I wanted the world to see just how special she was.

I would like to give thanks to all the people who helped me along the way, first my Mother, Willetta Neal for teaching me at an early age to follow my dreams and never give up.

To Pastor Wanda Williams my Spiritual Mother, and family friend who told me years ago,

"God said write this book. "

Smith McCann Jr. for his words of encouragement, listening ear and for teaching me to follow my dreams and not to settle for less.

To my sister Pastor Kim Dial my Best friend and Spiritual Partner in the Lord.

To My Husband Bishop Herbert Hucks for his word of encouragement both Spiritual and Naturally, for his listening ear, constructive criticism, and most of all his Love and Support. To my Children Sherita Neal, Smith McCann 111, Jeremiah Neal and all my grandbabies, who are my inspiration to press on and to let them know with God all things are Possible. To all who purchase this book, I hope it will bless you as much as it has Blessed me.

TABLE OF CONTENTS

ACKNOWLEDGMENTS   iii

ANGEL IN MY VIEW   1

CONTROL   4

TROUBLED TIME   6

JESUS CAN   8

INVITATION   10

HOLY SPIRIT   12

A MOTHER'S LOVE   14

IN LOVING MEMORY   16

FOR YOU MOTHER   18

RECEIPE FOR A BLESSED MARRIAGE   20

ADDICTION   22

SALVATION IS AT HAND   25

IN GOD WE TRUST   27

DO NOT FORGET   30

WITHOUT A PLAN   32

CELEBRATION   35

HOME GOING   37

IT'S TIME   39

FAREWELL   41

JOURNEY HOME   43

OUTSIDE   45

TAKE A CHANCE   47

MIND OVER MATTER   49

STAND   51

NEVER BE ASHAMED   52

MOTHER'S CRI'   54

MY M.V.P.   56

THROUGH THE EYE OF A CHILD   57

I CAN'T   58

RUMORS   60

GOOD TIMES   62

FALLEN   64

THE RACE   66

THE OTHER PERSON   68

FREEDOM   70

COMPROMISE   71

A GUN WITHOUT A CONSCIENCE   73

WARNING   75

GOD KNOWS   77

B.I.B.L.E.   78

DON'T QUIT   80

PROVEN LOVE   83

Angel In My View

I had an Angel all along,
In my view I couldn't see it,
So, I never knew it

As I closed my eyes,
the tears began to flow
I thought, can anyone see me,
don't they know?

The pain and suffering
and what I had to endure
They say fight, be strong,
but I don't know how for sure

I was so independent,
I always stood on my own
I thought I could do it,
So, I wanted to be left alone

But when I needed help,
no one was there
I cried many nights,
but it seemed that no one cared

I had no one to talk to,
no one to call
Whose arm could I lean on?
Who would catch me when I fall?

I had an Angel in my view,
So, wrapped into me,
that I couldn't see

Please forgive me JESUS
I never knew how much
you truly loved me
Until you sent an Angel
to comfort and set me free

There are angels that God sent
to cross my path
Maybe for a second, a moment, an hour
or for however long it lasted

I know now God sends his Angels
to help us along our way
And for this I thank him everyday

He does this to let us know
He loves us and He cares
To let us know we are never alone
He is always there

So, when you see someone
with outstretched hands
Be careful it may be God
Or an Angel who sees and understands

That you could not do it alone,
and needed God's help
To face the struggle head on,
and to complete the steps

See God will send His Angel,
to help you complete the task
For he was always there,
So, all you had to do was ask

So, see be careful
you could be entertaining
Angels unaware
So put your trust in JESUS,
for He loves you and He cares.

Control

For all the times I tried my best
to make things work out
For all the times we argued,
instead of talking it out

What was right or what was wrong,
only time will tell
What we should have done,
or what caused it to fail

Actions they say speak
louder than words
And proof would have made
a believer out of me
Never trying always saying
what happened was meant to be

I believe in life you can go as far
as you dare to dream
Even with life's ups and downs
things are not as bad as they seem

I know without a doubt
that all things are possible with God
In Him there is a sure win,
no matter what the odds

I know that life is not a guarantee
and you never know what tomorrow will bring
But it sure makes life more livable
knowing God is in control of everything

Troubled Time

When the burdens lay heavy
on my shoulders
Lord have mercy and strengthen me

When the way becomes cloudy
and I can no longer see
Your promises or the path
you have set for me

When tears flow more freely
and the way seems to be bad
Encourage my heart Lord,
for you are the lifter of my head

When my mind is struggling within itself,
and I feel so alone
Help me to remember
that there is always a Ram in the bush
To remind me that
I am not on my own

Lord send your Peace
as only you can do
For it is not my will,
but it is all about you

Help me not to lose sight of
what my purpose is in life
For I am a willing vessel,
whether day or night

Praising you Lord
through the good and bad
Honor and obey,
following what the word said

For I am Blessed,
for my Father said so
I'll take Him with me,
no matter where I go

Thank you JESUS
for the shedding of your blood

Jesus Can

Lord, why do you still have mercy
after all the things I have done
Why do you take out the time or even bother
with this old sinful man and all that I get into

Now I was so confused,
I did not know where to go or what to do
I never knew someone could love me
so unconditionally

I never knew my heart could feel so free
I heard people talking about this man called
Jesus and still did not understand

Until I took timeout for myself
to learn about this man
Oh! How great was this man
who had my best interest at heart
Who proved to be someone I could trust
and who would never depart

He said I love you
and I felt it deep within
He said He could
heal me and deliver me from sin.

All I had to do was confess
and believe in my heart that
He would wash away all my sins
and give me a new start

I listened closely to what he told me
and I knew in my heart it was true
I was so excited
I could not wait
to do what He asked me to do

So overwhelmed with joy,
I wanted to tell everyone I saw
About this man called Jesus
who washed and made me clean
I love you Lord Jesus
for all you have done
He said, "You are welcome,
and I love you too my son."

Invitation

What must I do
to know this man called Jesus Christ?
What must I do
to have him in my life

I am glad you asked'
I will be glad to show you the way
Once you follow these steps,
your life will never be the same

It will be for the better
and this you will see.
For you were once bound by sin,
but now you are free

First ask for God forgiveness
of all your sins
Repent with a Godly sorrow
and invite Him in

Making Him Lord and Savior of your life
and determine in your heart to live right
Being baptized of the water and of the spirit,
walking in the newness of life

You will go down a sinner,
but rise up a Child of the King
For you are now a child of God
and the angels rejoice and sing.

You must turn from the old way
and walk in the way that's right
And of course, the devil is not happy,
So, he will begin to fight

He will try to come against you
with everything he knows to do
Just pray and do not give up,
for my God will see you through

Yes, the road gets a little rough
and the hills hard to climb
But you are a Child of the King now,
so everything will be fine

Always read the word of God (Bible)
for this is your instruction of life
The devil cannot hurt you,
his bark is worse than his bite

And always remember
God is in control
and your battle He will fight.

Holy Spirit

I heard others talking
and I just could not believe
That was all it took
in order to receive

The gift of God is eternal life
and there are steps we must take
You must tum from your sinful ways
and what you used to do
Put your trust in JESUS,
and let him lead you

Yes, you will be tempted and tried,
so was Jesus Christ
But that's when you have to be strong,
standing for what is right

See I heard the knock at my heart
and decided to let Him in
I accepted Jesus as my Lord and Savior,
And He became my life-long friend

I received the gift of the Holy Ghost,
now I'm covered by his blood
Now I am no longer my own
and I being showered in his love

From that moment on
my life was never the same
I am now a new creation
and baptized in Jesus Name

Down in the water,
raised in the newness of life
Rejoicing with my Savior Jesus Christ

Thanking him for the Precious Holy Ghost
who teaches me along the way
For when I felt like giving up.
It stepped in and made the day

So, all glory and honor belongs to JESUS,
for making my life complete
For it is my reservation
for a place in His Kingdom
Kneeling at His Feet

A Mother Love

I have the best Mother's Love
It's the Love,
that is a Blessing from above

Out of all the problems
that I have put you through
I just want you to know that
I will always Love you

I have realized that your Love is like no other
That's why I know that you're the perfect mother
I know I haven't been the best son
But you always made me feel like
the perfect one

We have had our ups and downs
You've always been there
In my time of need,
you always stay around

You've always come to me
with the perfect advice
Even though I didn't show it,
those words made me think twice

I want you to know you're never unappreciated
I'm grateful to have you for a mother
I'll never trade you for another

So, every night when I pray,
I thank God above
For giving me an Angel as a Mother
with unconditional Love.

In Loving Memory

In memory of you
on this special day.
My heart is sadden
that you went away

For in my heart,
the pain still seems fresh
Sometimes it still doesn't seem real,
it's as if you never left

I wish I could feel your touch,
just once more
I wish I could hear your voice,
as I open the door

I ask myself,
"Is this really happening to me?"
Why did you have to go?
Why did you have to leave?

I know you tried to be strong,
to keep up a good fight
The suffering is now over
Knowing you're at peace, makes it alright

I have my memories to last a lifetime,
and they can't be erased
There is no one like you,
no one can ever take your place

For I know God only takes the best
That why he called you home,
now take your rest.

With all my love
Happy Mother Day!

For You Mother

To all the real Mothers,
that we sometime forget
A Super Woman,
who has never failed us yet

The Matriarch of the Family,
the glue that keep us strong
A strong arm of discipline,
when we choose to do wrong

A fountain of wisdom,
a wealth of knowledge to be learned
The tears, the struggles, the sacrifices,
"World's Best Mother" you've earned

I look in the mirror
and thank God above
For a real Mother,
full of unconditional love

Always so quick to give to others,
all that she has
But she never lets you know it,
even when it was her last

I've been blessed with a real Mother,
and I salute her today
A Mentor, A Friend,
a Mother in every way

May God continue to bless you,
"Happy Mother's Day!"

Recipe For A Blessed Marriage

Ingredients

Shower of Blessing
Abundance of Prayer
Pan of Honesty
Abundance of Love
Cup of Fasting
Cup of Faith
Stick of Understanding
Bag of Laughter
Stick of Peace
Bowl of Mercy
Abundance of Patients

In a bowl of Mercy,
combine an Abundance of Love,
and a stick of Understanding,
A cup of Faith, a little laughter,
followed by a hardy helping of Prayer,

Mix well with the Stick of Peace.

Let set for 5 to 10 minutes,
giving Ingredients time to blend

Now take a pan of Honesty
and line with a Layer of Love
with a ½ stick of Understanding

Combine remaining Ingredients in pan,
let cook for 45 to an Hour.

Don't forget to add a Cup of Fasting and Prayer.

Just make sure the cake is cooked properly
and will stand and not fall.

When complete,
you will have a Beautiful cake,
iced with Shower Of Blessing from above.

Making a Beautiful Marriage
and a Delicious Cake full of Love.

Addiction

You don't know me,
So, let me introduce myself
I will wine you and dine you
until there is nothing left

I can bring a strong man
to his knees
I can make a proud man
beg and plead

Just one taste of me,
you will be begging for more
I have you running around
like a kid in a candy store

Seconds/minutes/hours of pleasure,
can turn your world upside down
Have you feeling tall as a mountain,
but yet I'm pulling you to the ground

I come in all forms, shapes, sizes,
but yet pure as the driven snow
Why you choose to do it,
I really don't know

The temptation is great,
the desire so strong
you can't stop, you need it,
even though it was wrong

First, I talk to your mind,
and have you thinking all kinds of things
Then parodied sets in
and have you acting strange
The shakes, sniffing and scratching,
don't forget that

Now I've completed my purpose,
To You I take off my hat
In just one blow,
I have destroyed it all
You've lost your family,
friends and job,
Now, who can you call?

Remember me, they call me
'Addiction,'
yes, I am here to stay
Go on and get help,
go to the treatment center,
I'm not going away

Now, we all have heard and seen this story
So, many times before
They say there is no way out
and no open doors

But I know a man who says yes
when doctors say, "No way"
The one and only who shed his blood
that our souls could be saved

His name is JESUS,
and He Loves you
Just put your trust in Him,
he will see you through

Salvation Is At Hand

Do you think Heaven was mad
as thunder and lightning cracked the sky?
That was God's beloved son
who you crucified

He came that you might have life,
but you chose to Him die
Thieves, robbers you chose
letting truth pass you by

When it was all over
the light was gone
When did you come to your senses?
Realizing what you did was wrong?

You crucified innocent blood
His only crime was His love

For a Lack of Knowledge,
it is a shame
For Jesus Christ was His name

He came to earth
in the form of man
To bring peace and Salvation
to a dying Land

So, you thought it was over,
when you crucified Him
But the true Light of God,
you cannot hide

See you could not take his life,
for He laid it down
So that the path would be made plain,
and Salvation could be found

If you follow my example,
follow my lead
Your soul will be saved
and you will live in paradise with me.

In GOD We Trust

There is a harsh reality in this land today
People don't always do what they say

From minor to major, to say the least
As far as our natural arms can reach

From creed to promises, so many have been
said
Some are fulfilled and others make you mad

The one that stands out to me the most
Is the very same one that we post

It's in our Pledge, in our everyday life
and even in the currency we spend
It travels a lot of places
and have stood until the end

No it's not the American Flag,
but in God We Trust
If it is a part of us, then why all the fuss

Don't you see we are pushing it out,
as if it don't exist
But in time of trouble we call Him,
and then He becomes a must

God is real whether you believe it or not
We are living in troubled time
and it will not stop

The killing, stealing, robbing, to say the least
Some battle you will win,
and other will end in defeat

We have to open up our eyes
and look at the big picture ahead
For without GOD, we are already dead

No not Physically,
but your Spirit is lost
We must examine ourselves,
and count up the cost

I'm not trying to force God on you,
that's a choice you will have to make
I rather have God on my side,
than to make a mistake

But don't take my word,
try Him for yourself
With everything that's going on,
what do you have left?

We say 'In God We Trust,'
and treat him like someone we don't know
We say we love Him,
but are too ashamed to let it show

We pray sometimes,
read our Bible every now and then
And to say we are Christians,
now that would be a sin

Without God,
we won't make it down here
Men, Lack of Knowledge
is what brings about fear

For true victory is in God,
I hope someday this world will see
The Battle has already been won,
and we are now free.

Do Not Forget

Woke up this morning thinking
what I planned to do today
Rushing to get started
and knew I forgot to pray

Saying to myself, "I will do it,"
as I went on about my day
Knowing prayer is a must,
I cannot let anything stand in the way

Now sometimes things get a little rough,
like a lumberjack cutting trees
You will work up a sweat,
but once you get started, it is a breeze

But today for some reason,
no matter what I do
It like a dead end street,
I just can't get through

I look at this day
comparing to all others
Then I realized
I forgot to pray

But I knew who to call on
to unblock my path
Instantly I began to pray,
"Jesus please help,"
He said, "I am here my child
all you had to do is ask."

Without A Plan

We are a powerful nation,
United and free
But we do not understand
or even see

What we do to Our Nation
without God in the plan
We open the door for tragedy
and disaster in the land

Now Oklahoma bombing, 9/11,
and Katrina were all devastating
to go through
We cried out as a Nation,
asking what can we do?

We gave from our heart,
coming together in virtue and prayer
Jesus have mercy,
please cover us in your care

No prayer in school
and too ashamed in a public place
It is Jesus in time of trouble
and the rest of the time
we treat it as a disgrace

It's like teaching a lesson in school,
the learning up to you
It depends solely on how well you listen
and what you do

Some apply it to their everyday life
Some let it fall on deaf ear
with envy and strife

I do know one thing,
if you live long enough you will see
That Jesus is our only hope
when it comes to being free

So, in the time of trouble,
Who do you call?
What do you do?
I call on Jesus,
I know He will see me through

He is my everything
and when I need Him,
He is always there
I know He loves me and He cares

He will never leave me
or forsake me, this is true
I know who to call,
I know what He can do

Salvation is a gift if you want it,
that choice is up to you
Put your trust in Jesus,
He will see you through.

Celebration

It is a Party!
let's celebrate
Rejoice and enjoy,
for the news is great

It is a Homegoing,
announce it all over town
It is Finish,
I am with my Savior now

No more sad faces
or bowed heads
No more pain and suffering,
or tears to be shed

Beautiful white horses,
stepping high and proud
The Band playing,
The Choir singing aloud

Hallelujah, Thank you Jesus,
another child has made it in

The battle is now over,
I have victory over sin
I am reunited with my friends

Loved ones who went on before
I set my house in order
and my Spirit is on one accord

I could hear my Savior calling,
for my life down here would be no more
I closed my eyes
and peace came over my soul
I said, "Yes Lord, I am ready to go."

So, see no more sorrow
and no tears to shed
No regrets or bowed heads

Celebrate with me,
I am home with my Savior above
Rejoicing is His goodness
and resting in His Love.

Home Going

I could hear the angels singing
I could hear the saints praising His name
Another homecoming, hallelujah
we give Jesus the highest praise

It is then that I close my eyes
for I knew life down here
would be no more
My spirit is finally at peace,
resting on God celestial shores

It's not death, but life for me
I'm in the Master's arms,
and my soul is free.

Free to sing his praise
and rejoice in his love.
To take on my new building,
and reunite with the saints above.

I know everyone will miss me
and I'll miss them too.
This is a Divine Appointment
we all must keep something
we have to do.

I could hear the train of glory
my bags were packed and ready to go.
The angel shouted "Hallelujah"
my child this is your stop, all aboard.

I looked back to say goodbye to friends
and loved ones behind.
I didn't have a chance,
it wasn't enough time.

The whistle blew just once,
and like a vapor, we were gone.
I'm in a better place,
I'm finally home.

This is not the end
we will meet again someday.
On the other side in God's Kingdom
that's what the word of God does say.

I know you all loved me
but God loved me best.
He said welcome home my child,
It time to take your rest

It's Time

When you lose someone you love,
and don't know what to do
Nothing eases the pain,
And no one to comfort you

Hearts feel so heavy, eyes fill with tears
You ask the question,
How could this happen to someone
so close and so dear?

What will fill the empty place,
the void in my life?
How can I go on without them?
Will it ever be right?

They say that time will ease the emptiness
that I now feel
And by the grace of God
the wounds will begin to heal

God knows what he is doing,
He loves us one and all
Just put your faith in Him,
He'll be there when you call

For we know not the hour, or day
when the Son of God shall appear
But make no mistake,
for it's perfectly clear

Surely as you live,
you shall surely die
Choices in this life,
determines where you will lie

Choose God and live
or the world and die
So when death does come,
where will you abide
In the cares of the world
or with Jesus on the other side.

Farewell

There is another empty space
in our family circle
as we stand side by side
So, I will just say farewell
and not goodbye

You know you will be greatly missed
in every way
How could we forget,
that big bright smile that made our day.

The fun and laughter we shared,
all the family reunion along the years
How can we not miss you?
It would be hard not to shed some tears

Of course, we have the memory
we will cherish and hold dear
But it's still not the same
as having you here

We all have a Divine appointment
with our maker that we must keep
So farewell for now,
you are not dead but asleep.

We never know when it is our time,
or how we will go
But in God's Divine order
He calls His children home

No more pain and suffering,
we will finally be at rest
I know you all loved me
but God loved me best.

Journey Home

There is a Higher Power,
God is in control
He set a boundary for us all,
beyond it we cannot go

We ask so many times why
And a lot of things we don't understand
but God has the final say,
control is in His hand

Death is the beginning of Life
It makes the cycle complete
Some call it death,
but in God, it's called Sleep

The Word of God tells us
"Earth has no sorrow
that heaven can't heal"
He is a Merciful God
and your pain he feels

God dispatched his angels,
So, they would not be alone
To comfort his child in time of need,
and guide them safely home

For God saw fit to pick a Rose
from his garden of life
The memories shall live on,
although they're out of sight

So, it ok to cry,
but they're in a better place now,
This is a home going,
and His peace they have found

So, give praise to God,
rejoice with the Angels above
They're now with the Savior
and resting in his Love.

Outside

In the softness of the wind
a still voice can be heard
One of the Greatest mysteries,
the best story ever told

What makes the trees stand
so tall in the evening grass?
God's glorious riches unfold
as the evening passes

The peace that comes
with the soft and shuttle wind
Some of the Greatest wonders
that have stood since time began

The sun that shines
just enough to give us what we need
The rain that falls in due time
that supply and feed

God's hand of Love
that shades us when we need to rest
The joy in knowing He loves us
and gives us what is best

So, when you are outside and enjoying
whatever season comes your way
Remember to thank God above
for Blessing us with this day.

Take A Chance

In the mist of the storm,
there is a Ray of Light
That comes to let us know
everything will be alright

We think our situation is bad
and that maybe true
But when we think we have seen it all,
there is someone worse off than you

We are so quick to give up,
saying there is nothing left to do
But if you take time, and explore the options,
you'll see things will work out for you

We can only do so much,
so why worry about it
What you cannot change
We stress ourselves out
and the situation is still the same

You say you need a way out,
a new relief on life
I have the perfect plan
that will change the wrong to right

Learn to give thanks to God
first in everything you do.
Invite God in, give him control,
and let him direct you.

Give God his percentage,
your first fruit,
for it is right and true.
You will find peace,
you will be amazed
at how he will bless you

Stop saying what you cannot do,
Just step out on faith
Put your trust in God,
he always makes a way.

Mind Over Matters

Lord, open my mind,
expand my views
Help me look beyond the circumstances
Help me to see only you

I have lost sight of reality in life
I have tried everything else,
I can get our hands on
Instead of choosing what is right

Please search my heart
for all the unclean things
Help me to accept
whatever the search brings

Sometimes we say we are tired,
we want a change to take place
But we are so quick to give up,
before we start the race

We kneel in position and
lose sight of the finish line
And before we know it,
we are alone and left behind

You look around to shift the blame,
but there is only you
Now who's fault is it,
what are you going to do?

You can give up,
like so many before you
Or put your trust in God,
for he guides you safely through

Remember this is a battle,
we must fight and be strong
For with God as your Personal trainer,
you can't go wrong.

Stand

Standing on the Battlefield
full of anger and despair.
There suddenly appeared an Angel
out of nowhere.

Saying, "Why fight a battle this way,
when you know it not right?"
Satan's not after the flesh and blood,
But your spirit that shines bright.

For only what we do for Christ   lasts,
this one thing is true.
The Victory is already yours,
so be careful what you do.

Satan desires to swift as wheat,
But God will see you through.
There is nothing he can do,
the door has been shut tight
Your Heavenly father has the key
and the Battle He will fight

So stop holding your head down,
and walk strong in the Lord
For you are His Child,
who He Loves and Adores.

Never Be Ashamed

Why is the world so ashamed?
Who is this man
that they keep calling his name
They say his name is Jesus Christ

How He came in
and changed their life
How He picked them up
when they were down
How he cleaned their lives up,
set them on solid ground

In their time of trouble
He is always there
When that so call friend
lets you down,
He shows He cares

So, why when it comes
to praising his name
We know we are at fault,
but others we blame

Our mouth gets tight
and our voices get low
When it comes time
to let the world know

To open your mouth
and Thank him for what He has done
For the Little Blessings
as well as the Big ones

Always give praise
to the Head of our Life
Our Lord and Savior
JESUS CHRIST!!!!

Mother's Cri'

I love you, I love you,
I love you, I love you

When the tears begin to flow
and you are feeling sad and blue
Remember these words,
keep them in your heart,
for they are true

I wish I could freeze time
and change the wrong to right
I wish I could be there
one more time
to kiss you goodnight

There will always be a ray of sunshine
to light your way
There will always be
warm hugs and kisses
to start your day

Look deep into your heart,
there you will find me
It's there I have always been
and there I will always be

When you think of me,
you will feel my love overflow
I did not get to tell you
as much as I like,
but I hope you always know

You were my life,
I hope you understand and see
I am absent in body,
but I live on in memory

So, I asked the Lord
to send his Angels from above
To guide your footsteps
and shower you with his love

To ease the pain
and wipe away all the tears
And to keep you now and forever,
and protect you in the coming years.

My M.V.P.

Your eyes were always watching,
but I never knew
That the M.V.P.
(Most Valuable Person)
would be you

My Protector, My Queen,
My Angel from above
My number one,
full of unconditional Love

I know I've made mistakes,
but you never left my side
When I seem to lose my way,
you were there to guide

You taught me how to stand,
and now I'm on my own
You're my Mother,
I'll always be your child,
even when I'm grown

A one of a kind Mother,
Special in every way
I love you now and forever
Happy Mother's Day!

Through The Eye Of A Child

It takes a special person to be a Mother,
this I know is true
Caring, loving, understanding,
nurturing, one of a kind, that's you

If I owned the world,
I would serve it to you
on a plate of gold

For a true Mother is a Queen,
a story to be told
Living an Ordinary life,
but she is true royalty in every way

She gives her last for her family,
the sacrifices made every day
She never complains,
always in the right place at the right time

A rare and precious jewel, like a star,
she forever shines
A vision of beauty,
a work of art
You'll always be special
for you hold the key to my heart

I Can't

Lord I can't go on,
I can't take another step
My heart is so heavy,
what do I have left

I don't understand,
I can't see
How you could take someone
so precious to me

You of all people knew
what he meant to me
How could this happen?
How could this be?

I will never see him again,
or hear his voice
I'm so overwhelmed with pain,
like a hit with great force

Lord please help me,
Please lift my pain
My life from this point on
will never be the same.

Jesus Said,
"I gave him to you,
but only for a little while
To help watch over him,
but he's still my child
I created him,
his soul belongs to me

I know you may not understand now
But in time you will see
I know you loved him,
but My Love outweighs it all
I'm the one who gave him life,
I make the final call

The Trauma was too much for his body,
I had to retrieve his soul
And about you Love,
Yes I do know

The pain, the tears,
I know how you feel
But earth has no sorrow,
that I the Heavenly Father can't heal"

Rumors

It starts out as a little rumor,
that could bring a kingdom down
It's such a juicy story,
you will spread it around

It starts off as one thing
and ends up being two or three
I told you this was a good one,
now tell someone for me

You know good news just sets,
but bad news travel fast
They tell it with such pride
and the result are a blast

Someone who has it all together,
strong and standing tall
Is now shaking and trembling,
like a ton of bricks, they fall

You laugh, point fingers and say
"I told you they are not all that"
You get such joy in others pain,
you even make bets

But there is something
they forgot to tell you,
you should have known
My life belong to JESUS,
and I am no longer my own

So the rumors you spread
that you thought had brought me down
Just made me pray harder,
for I stand on solid ground

Yes rumors hurt
and can sometimes shake your soul
But there is still something you forgot,
you act as you don't know

JESUS is the watchman,
he protects my soul
I never have to worry,
for my help comes from above
I found safety in his arms,
for I'm covered by his blood.

Good Times

Why is it so dark in here?
What have I entered in
Welcome my little worker
into the world of sin

There will be parties and dancing
that last all night
There will be food and drinks
to make you feel just right

There will be men and women
whichever one suits your taste
Welcome again to the world of sin,
this is a happy place

They say the fun is out of this world,
with benefits to die for
Once you enter in,
there is no more open door

For the wages of Sin is Death
and that is what you will receive
Unless you turn from the world of sin,
trust JESUS and believe

There will be parties and dancing,
but to a different beat
For the D.J. is Doctor Jesus
and he sits in the Mercy Seat.

There will be light instead of darkness,
this you will plainly see
Once you enter Club Divine
the shackles are broken
and you are free

Free to sing and dance
and shout praises to God above
For His divine deliverance
and His Shower of Love
And thanks again
for the Invitation to the party
and the introduction to the club

Fallen

Please do not be so quick to judge me
by the situations or circumstances I am in
Pray for me if I have backslidden
or fallen into sin

I have fallen short
of what God has planned for me today
Because I took my eyes off of Him
and went my own way

I know the Lord,
and what he has chosen me to do
I have lost my direction,
Lord please help me make it through

I have become entangled in my own lust
I have done what I wanted to do,
instead of what I must

Forgive me Lord,
for what I do or say
We have all fallen short,
So, help us not to judge but pray

Pray for one another
for we don't know
what a person's going through
Help us Lord
to focus on what we must do

Lord, I love you with all my heart
In your will
I want to stay and never depart

I'm sorry for my short comings
and mistakes along the way
Please take control
and give me a clean heart today

He said, "Come my child
let me wash away your sins
Make you white as snow,
and the healing can begin

In the sea of forgetfulness
is where they will stay
Put your trust in me,
and I will show the way."

The Race

I am preparing for a race
that sometimes gets difficult to run
The path is not easy
and it is not all fun

There are many paths to choose,
the choice is up to you
What you say and do,
determines if you will make it through

A little faith in God,
as a grain of a mustard seed
A lot of praying
and the Bible you must read

For we have to be prepared
for every course that comes our way
Then we will be ready for that big day

I have a Personal trainer
preparing me for the race
He told me, exactly what to do
and he sets the pace

He said, "Get ready, Get ready!
this race we all must run"
The stop watch went off
and the race begun

I raced out of position
and down the lane I went
I called on the name of Jesus
and toward heaven I sent

All my prayers and requests,
Crying, "Lord hear my call"
Thanking him for preparing me,
and for not letting me fall

Give me the strength of Samson
and help me not to die
Give me your shoe of fire
with power from on high

This is a Spiritual race
that we all will run someday
Jesus give us our instructions
and shows us the way

The race is not for the swift or strong,
but to the one who endures to the end
So, who will prepare you
and will Lose or Win!

The Other Person

In all my days of living,
I never thought it would happen to me
All of the signs and warnings,
I did not see

All the years together
through the good and bad,
Now what am I to do?
How do I face the rest of my life
knowing I won't have you?

In the late night hour
I reach for you
but you're not there
In my lonely times,
who will comfort me,
and who will care?

Earth has no sorrow
that heaven cannot heal.
Jesus knows every one of our hurts,
He knows how you feel

He knows I love you
and how much you love me too
But this is something
we all must go through

As sure as we live,
we shall surely die
There is no way around it,
no way to get by

So we must live each day
as if it's our last
Doing the Master's will,
doing what he asks

Keeping His commandment,
hiding them in our hearts
Praying daily without fail,
making life with Christ an art

A Beautiful Masterpiece
for others to see
A window of beautiful blessings,
how life should be

And when that time comes,
you can close your eyes
and take your rest
Knowing you are resting in the Lord,
it is there you are truly blessed.

Freedom

In harm's way
you placed your life
As a sheep to the slaughter,
the perfect sacrifice

No greater Love
that You gave for me
To take on the sin of the world,
that I may be free

For I have not always done
what you asked of me
I have made so many mistakes,
but you still had mercy

To still Love me
in the mist of all my sins
To forgive me
and still welcome me in

I Love you Lord,
because you first love me
It is in you I have life
and can truly be free.

Compromise

I chose you to preach my word
uncompromising and true
So, why do you choose to follow the people
and do what you want to do?

But Lord I know what your word said,
I just wanted to put a little fun in it
I added a little of my own ideals
so the message I gave would fit

The people really loved it,
they clapped and said "Amen"
I really think they like me now,
we have become friends

"It's not about you my child,
my will must be done"
What about their soul salvation
and the uncompromising truth my son"

I am sorry Lord
I know what I done was not right
I just tried to give them
what they wanted to hear
or what I thought they would like

"But I chose you to preach my word
uncompromising and true
You are going to make some enemies
and some people will not like you

You have to feed my people
and tell them what my word says
For if you do not
their blood will be required of you this day

You will be held accountable for the souls lost
All because you did not preach the truth
and tell them about the cross
How I died and shed my blood
for the remission of their sin

How they can be saved
and how they can make it in
Now go my son, make haste and do
what I have called you to do
My sheep are going astray
and they need our help to make it through.

A Gun Without a Conscience

A gun doesn't have a conscience
Nor Bullet eyes
It will hit any and everything in its path
It has no guide

A life changing tragedy
It will kill the mortal soul
They are dangerous, especial in the wrong hands
We are killing one another
We're the worst enemy to man

So quick to anger,
Never stopping to think
If animals are endangered species
Then mankind will soon be extinct

At the rate we're going
The value of life
No rational thinking
Never choosing what is right

Whatever happened to saying I'm sorry
When things go wrong
Always having the last word
Instead of forgiving and going on

What's so bad to make you kill
Within seconds life has come to an end

Not to mention the pain and suffering
What about the family and friends?
What about the Parent(s)?
How do you think they will feel?
To get a call or knock on the door
Saying their loved one has been killed

In such a brutal way
Sometimes words can't explain
The pain, heaviness of the heart
Life will never be the same

So, when you pull out your gun
Think, is this right?
Picture your Parent's face
Being snatched from their life
Think how great the pain and loss
Will they be able to endure?

This is someone's baby
It could be you
Now asked yourself, 'Are You Sure?'

Warning

Heaven gates are closing
Why do you not come in?
How long will you take life for granted and live in
sin?
You hear the voice of the Lord
But you won't take heed
Why do you choose bondage?
When you can be free

Things may look good now
Everything's going your way
When happens when your plans for tomorrow
Becomes Today?
The Word of God says, 'take no thought for
tomorrow'
For it is not promised to use
So, why do you choose the easy way out
Instead of what you must
So wrapped up within ourselves
Forgetting about God above

Think you've got it going on
Missing out on God's perfect love

For the wages of sin is death
Life will come to an end
Then who can you call on?
Who can you depend?

So, why not take heed before it's too late
The choice we make in life will determine our fate

So, you can choose to die in the world of sin
Or give your life to God and eternal life,
You Will Win!

God Knows

Tried and murdered
What did I do wrong?
Judged by the color of my skin
As if I didn't belong

Race is not a factor
This is what the voices say
But I have no voice and
Here is where I lay

Absent from my family, friends
Whose face I will see no more
Why is the question I ask?
Why did this happen to me?

Victory you think you've won
Because things went your way
It may be over for now
But there will be a Judgement Day

Never escaping, for what you reap
You will sow
You can fool the people
But just remember, God knows!!

B.I.B.L.E.

We are living the B.I.B.L.E.
You and me
Stop, listen, look around and
You will see

The signs of the time are
Right before your eyes
Whether right or wrong
We are in control of our lives

We preach our own funeral
In the life we live
Salvation is not granted
By the service you give

But by Repenting
Asking for forgiveness from God
Become a real vessel
Even if it seems odd

See how your life will change
Forget about what people say
Contrary to Popular belief
There is no other way

So, if you are a sinner
This is your way out
A chance to come into the Knowledge of God

Find out what JESUS is all about
And if you are saved,
Filled with the Holy Ghost from above
Then you have eternal life
You are now covered in His Blood

See there is nothing new under the sun
What once was has now become
Different era, a different name
Different generation, but the same thing

Read the Bible
You will see
How it happened
How it came to be

There is no situation
That the Bible doesn't speak of
Different authors
But still directed from above

To write about the greatest stories to ever be told
To encourage and instruct
The young and the old

You can't go wrong, when you read and follow it
It will set you free
The Bible, The Way of Life
Salvation for you and me

Don't Quit

My heart is truly saddened
For our youth today
No one takes time to them
There is a better way

They are always on the move
There is no easy way out
You have to work to get ahead
I know what I'm talking about

The guns, drugs and fast money
Are all materials things
You'll never get to enjoy it
Look at the consequences it brings

Always on edge, looking over your shoulder
Even with your ride or die around
Bullet has no eyes
When it's all over you are going down

Who's standing with you now
Will your ride or die take the fall?
If you're not dead by now
You'll be fingerprinted and booked
With you back against the wall

Wake up Youth
It's not the world's fault
If you have not learned by now
Then it's time to be taught

Nothing beats a failure but a try
Life is worth living and
You don't have to die

It's time to stand up
Stop following the crowd
Telling yourself you're worth more
You are somebody
Shout it out loud

Let me introduce you to someone
Who knows you better than you know yourself
He'll be there when you need Him
Even when you feel there's nothing left

His name is JESUS
He came to give us life and that more abundantly
Because of the shedding of His Blood
We are now free

For no greater Love I have found
Than the Love He has for me
Don't take my word for it
Try Him for yourself and you will see

He looked beyond my faults and
He saw my needs
He turned my life around
He saw what I could be

So, you see there is a way out
It's time to come clean
Show this world what you are all about

You're Blessed., For the God you serve
Our Father is King
He is the Creator
He knows everything

So, we as parents have to keep up the fight
"DON'T QUIT'
Because anything broken
With JESUS it can be fixed

PROVEN LOVE

Another Sunday in church
Men I'm tired of this
Sitting here doing nothing
On this hard bench

What is the purpose?
Why did I have to go?
Because I as a child, no one listened to me
I wished they could understand
Or at least see

Now my Mother always kissed and said,
"You'll understand in time."
What you learn now will guide you in life
You will be fine

I still did not understand
And time just went on
And before I knew it
I was grown and on my own

I never forgot the words my Mother said
All the things I heard,
Are now planted in my head

As time went on,
I remember what she instilled in me
She said, "My child, keep Jesus in your life
You'll need Him, you will see"

A situation arose and
I could not see my way out
Then I remembered the Man
My Mother taught me about

Instantly I feel to my knees
And began to pray
Jesus, please help me
I need you today

My Mother taught me about you
And now I need you for myself
I have nowhere to turn
You are all I have left

I heard your cry my child
I was waiting for you
Put your trust in me
I will see you through

I know the road has been bump
The hill hard to climb
But with Devine direction
You will be just fine

Thank you JESUS for have mercy and
Helping me to see
My shortcomings and
What I can be

JESUS I am ready now
To do what I must
It's in your hands
I put my complete trust.

Made in the USA
Middletown, DE
24 November 2018